A

PROJECT

FOR

FLYING.

In Earnest at Last!

Price, TWENTY-FIVE CENTS.

NEW YORK:
A. W. MACDONALD, Jr. & CO., PRINTERS,
32 Beekman Street.
1871.

A PROJECT FOR

FLYING.

In Earnest at Last!

A Project for Flying.

In Earnest at Last.

The following appeared in one of our public journals of the date indicated ·

To the Editor of the Tribune.

Sir:—You rightly appreciate the interest with which the popular mind regards all efforts in the direction of navigating the air.

One man of my acquaintance was deeply interested to know the results of the California Experiment, because he alone, as he believed, had questioned Nature and learned from her the great secret of aerial navigation.

To-day's *Tribune* brings us the full account of the machine, its performance and *modus operandi ;* and without the authority of my friend, I can pronounce at once that the thing is simply ridiculous. It is the same old useless effort, with the same impossible agents. But to-day, within twenty miles of Trinity steeple, lives the man who can give to the world the secret of navigating the air, in calm or in storm, with the wind or against it ; skimming the earth, or in the highest currents, just as he wills, with all the ease, and all the swiftness, and all the exactitude of a bird.

My friend is only waiting for an opportunity to perfect his plan, when he will make it known.

Yours truly,

W. H. K.

New York, June 14th, 1869.

Two years have passed and no progress has been made in aeriel navigation.

The California Experiment failed. The great Air-ship "City of New York," had previously escaped the same fate, only because more prudent than her successor she declined a trial. The promising and ambitious enterprise of Mr. Henson has hardly been spoken of for a quarter of a century. And notwithstanding the fact that the number of ascensions in balloons in the United States and Europe must be counted by thousands, and although the exigencies of recent wars have made them useful, yet it must be confessed that the art of navigating the air remains in much the same state in which the brothers Mont-golfiers left it at the close of the last century.

The reason for this want of progress in the art referred to, is not to be sought in any want of interest in the subject, or of enthusiasm in prosecuting experiments. Certainly not for want of interest in the subject, because *to fly*, has been the great desideratum of the race since Adam. And we find in the literature of every age suggestions for means of achieving flight through the air, in imitation of birds; or for the construction of ingenious machines for aerial navigation. And if history and traditions are to be credited, it would be equally an error to suppose that our age alone had attempted to put theory into practice in reference to navigating the air.

Even the fables of the ancients abound with stories about flying: that of Dedalus and his son Icarius, will occur to every reader. And the representations of the Poets, and the allusions in Holy Writ equally prove how natural and dear to the mind of man is the idea of possessing "wings like a dove."

But it is safe enough to assert, that hitherto, all attempts at *navigating* the air have been failures.

Floating through the atmosphere in a balloon,

at the mercy not only of every *wind* but of every *breath* of air, is in no adequate sense aerial navigation. And I do not hesitate to say, that balloons are absolutely incapable of being directed.

All the analogies by which inventors have been encouraged in their expectations are false, the rudders of ships and the tails of birds are no exceptions. They will never be able to guide balloons as sailors do ships, by a rudder, because ships do not float suspended in the water as balloons float in the air; nor do birds *float* through the air in any sense. They are not bouyant—lighter than the element in which they move, but immensely heavier; besides they do not guide themselves wholly by their tails. We may depend upon it, if we ever succeed in navigating the air, it will be by a strict adherence to the principles upon which birds fly, and a close imitation of the means which they employ to effect that object.

It is true, that in respect to the means to be employed, animals designed by the Creator for flight, have greatly the advantage of us, but what natural deficiencies will not human ingenuity supply, and what obstacles will not human skill overcome? It has already triumphed over much greater than any that Nature has interposed between man and the pleasures of aerial communication.

We have to a great extent, mastered the mysterious elements of nature.

We have conquered the thunderbolt and learned to write with the burning fluid out of which it is forged.

We have converted the boundless ocean into a vast highway, traversed for our use and on our errands, by the swift agent, and by great ships driven against wind and tide by the mighty power of steam.

And yet a single generation ago, we knew nothing

of all this, Our grand-sires would have given these achievements a prominent place in the list of impossible things.

But, do you say, "the Creator never intended us to fly—*therefore*, it is impossible."

For what did the Creator give us skill and boundless perseverance? Was it designed that we should *swim*, more than that we should furnish ourselves with wings and mount up as eagles? "We sink like lead in the mighty waters," we only fall a little faster through the air.

Still, I grant that the problem of aerial navigation will only be solved when the principles of flight are clearly understood, and we recognize precisely what are the obstacles which prevent us from flying by artificial means.

Will these obstacles prove insuperable? It is at present believed by the multitude that they will, but I entertain a different opinion, most decidedly.

From my earliest youth this subject has occupied my thoughts. It has been the study of my life, and I modestly trust that I have not questioned nature and science in vain.

In the first place, I undertook to make myself familiar with the obstacles to be overcome. I found the greatest of these to be gravity. I found, however, that heavy fowls, who were unable to rise *from the earth*, and only accomplished flight by taking advantage of an eminence, sustained themselves without difficulty when once fairly embarked. I also found that the best flyers were not equal to the feat of keeping me company, when walking at my usual pace; hence I inferred that *velocity* was a necessary element in flight, and that gravity, so fatal to human attempts to fly, might be made a powerful auxiliary when rightly used.

Acting upon this hint, I made experiments with heavy barn yard fowls, and finally constructed a light apparatus to be operated by myself, using, principally, my feet as a motive power, which I repeatedly tried with various and *constantly increasing* degrees of success.

Now I am satisfied that my system is right. It is my sober conviction that the time to realize the dream and hope of ages has come. Startling as the announcement may be, I propose not only to make short excursions through the air myself, but to teach others to do the same.

Yet, knowing perfectly the obstacles in the way of flight, and knowing equally well how to overcome them, I am yet well aware that I must perfect my knowledge by practice before entire success can be achieved.

This is only reasonable.

How was it with the swimmer; how was it with the agile and dexterous skater; how with the acrobat, and what but practice has just enabled WESTON to walk one hundred and twelve miles in twenty-four hours, and four hundred miles in five days?

For want of a better name, I will call the machine upon which I am to practice, the "Instructor." It is simple, but it gives the learner just what he wants—an endless series of *inclined planes.*

It will prevent accidents, and until the student has mastered the mechanical movements necessary to flight, will supplement his efforts by partially balancing his weight.

It consists of a beam fifty feet long, poised and attached by a universal joint to the top of a form post, say twenty feet or more in height. Upon one end of this beam the practitioner stands, arrayed in his wings.

A movable weight at the other end completes the apparatus; and yet this simple machine, will form the entering wedge to aerial navigation.

And now methinks I see you smile, but, my unbelieving friends, let me remind you that COPERNICUS, and GALILEO, and FRANKLIN, and FULTON, and MORSE, —all better men than your humble servant, were laughed at before me.

Their work is done. Their monuments stand in all lands, and yet *one* of this band of truly great and worthy names still lives, and to him I am indebted for many kind and encouraging words.

It is little besides this that I ask of *you.* The stock which you are solicited to take in this enterprise is small. But enable me by your patronage to devote myself for a time wholly to my project. See to it, that I do not fail for want of support. Buy my little pamphlet at its insignificant cost, ask your friends to do so; and should any of you wish to contribute anything more to this cause, which I have made my own, and which I am determined to push to a triumphant issue, he may be sure that he will receive the acknowledgments of a grateful and earnest man, who has himself devoted to it the aspirations and efforts of a long life, and who is still willing to take all the risks of failure upon himself.

The undersigned would be pleased to have friends interested in this subject, call upon him, when the matter will be more fully described.

ROBERT HARDLEY,

17 PERRY STREET, or

114 Sixth Ave., cor. 9th St.

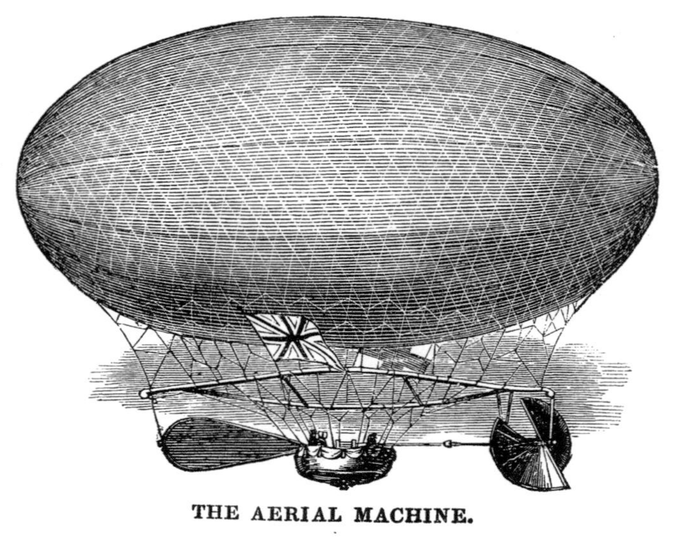

THE AERIAL MACHINE.

REMARKS

ON THE

ELLIPSOIDAL BALLOON,

PROPELLED BY THE

Archimedean Screw,

DESCRIBED AS THE

NEW AERIAL MACHINE,

NOW EXHIBITING AT THE

ROYAL ADELAIDE GALLERY,

LOWTHER ARCADE, STRAND.

LONDON:
PRINTED BY HOWLETT AND SON,
10, FRITH STREET, SOHO.

REMARKS, &c.

The object proposed in the construction of the Machine which is here presented to the public view, is simply to illustrate and establish the fact, that, by a proper disposition of parts and the application of a sufficient power, it is possible to effectuate the propulsion or guidance of a Balloon through the air, and thus to prepare the way for the more perfect accomplishment of this most interesting and desirable result.

In the contrivance of this design, one of the first effects aimed at was to reduce the resistance experienced by the Balloon in its progress, which is greater or less according to the magnitude and shape of its opposing surface. To this intent is the peculiar *form* of the Balloon, which is an *Ellipsoid* or *prolate spheroid,* the axis of which is twice its minor diameter; in other words, twice as long as it is broad. By this construction, the opposition to the progress of the Balloon in the direction of either end is only one *half* of what it would be, had it been a Balloon of the ordinary spherical form and of the same diametrical magnitude. For the exact determination of this proportion we are more particularly indebted to the researches of Sir George Cayley, a distinguished patron of the art, who, a few years back, instituted a series of experiments with a view to ascertain the comparative amounts of resistance developed by bodies of different forms in passing through the air; the results of which he communicated to the world in an essay first published in the Mechanic's Magazine, and afterwards in a separate pamphlet. According to these experiments it appears, that the opposition which an ellipsoid or oval (of the nature of the Balloon, if we may so call it, in the model) is calculated to encounter in proceeding *endways* through the atmosphere is only *one-sixth* of what a *plane* or *flat* surface of equal area with its largest vertical section, would experience at the same rate; while the resistance to the progress of a globe, such as the usual Balloon, would be one third of that due to a similar circular plane of like diameter: shewing an advantage, in respect of diminished resistance, in favour of the former figure, to the extent we have above described; an advantage it enjoys along with an increased capacity for containing gas—the cubical contents of an ellipsoid of the proportions here observed, being exactly double of those of an ordinary Balloon of equal diameter, and consequently competent to the support of twice the weight.

Independent of the advantage of reduced resistance in this form, there is another of nearly, if not quite, equal importance, in the facility it affords of directing its course; an object scarcely, if at all, attainable with a Balloon of the usual description, however powerfully invested with the means of motion; as any one will readily perceive who has ever noticed or experienced the difficulty, or rather the impossibility, of guiding a tub afloat in the water, compared with the condition of a boat or other similarly constructed body, in the same element. The efficacy of this provision and its necessity will appear more forcibly when we observe that whenever the Balloon in the machine here described is thrown out of its direct bearing by the shifting of the net-work which connects it with the hoop, or by any other accident whereby its position is altered with respect to the propelling power, its course is immediately affected, and it ceases to progress in a straight line, following the direction of its major axis, unless corrected by the intervention of a sufficient rudder.

The second object, after establishing a proper form for the floating body, was to contrive a disposition of striking surface that should be able to realise the greatest amount of propulsive re-action, in proportion to its magnitude and the force of its operation, which it is possible to accomplish. To shew by what steps and in consequence of what reasoning this point was determined as in the plan adopted, would occupy considerably more space than the few pages we have to spare would admit of our devoting to it. Suffice it to say that of all the means of creating a resistance in the atmosphere capable of being applied to the propulsion of the Balloon, the Archimedean Screw was ascertained to be undoubtedly the best. It is true that by a *direct* impact or stroke upon the air, as for instance by the action of a fan, or the wafting of any *flat* surface at *right angles* to its own plane, the maximum effect is accomplished which such a surface is capable of producing with a given power. The mechanical difficulties, however, which attend the employment of such a mode of operation are more than sufficient to counterbalance any advantage in point of actual resistance which it may happen to possess; at least in any application of it which has hitherto been tried or proposed: so that here, as in the case of ships propelled by steam, the *oblique* impact obtained by the rotation of the striking surface is found to be the most conducive to the desired result; and of these, that arrangement which is termed the Archimedean Screw is the most effective.

The result aimed at, being the development of the greatest amount of re-action in the direction of the axis of revolution, it is not enongh to have determined the *general* character of the instrument to be employed; the proper disposition or inclination ol its parts becomes a question of the first importance. According as the *turns* of the screw are more or less oblique with respect to the air they strike or the axis on which they revolve, more or less of the resistance they generate by their rotation becomes *resolved,* as it is technically expressed, in the direction of the intended course: in other words, converted to the purpose in view, namely, the propulsion of the Balloon.

Our limited space here again prevents us from entering into a detail of the experiments by means of which the true solution of this question has been arrived at, and the proper angle determined at which the superficial spiral exercises the greatest amount of propulsive force of which such an engine is capable. These experiments have been chiefly carried on by Mr. Smith, the ingenious and successful adapter of this instrument to the propulsion of steam vessels, for a series of years, with the greatest care, and at a very considerable expense; and the result of his experience gives an angle of about 67° or 68° for the outer circumference of the screw, as that productive of the maximum effect; a conclusion which is further verified by the experiments of Sir George Cayley, of Mr. Charles Green, the most celebrated of our practical aeronauts, and others who have employed their attention upon the subject. This conclusion requires only one modification, which ought to be noticed; namely, that in cases of extreme velocity, the number of the angle may be still further increased with advantage, until an inclination of about 73° be obtained; when it appears any further advance in that direction is attended with a loss of power. With these facts in view, the impinging surface of the Archimedean Screw, in the model under consideration, has been so disposed as to form, at its outer circumference, an angle of 68° with the axis of revolution, gradually diminishing as it approaches the centre, according to the essential character of such a form of structure.

The novelty of the application of this instrument to the propulsion both of ships and balloons, suggests the propriety of a few more explanatory remarks to elucidate its nature and meet certain objections which those who are ignorant of its peculiar qualities are apt to raise in respect of it.

Previous to the adoption of this particular instrnment, various analogous contrivances had been resorted to in order to produce the same effects. Of these, examples are afforded in the sails of the windmill, the vane of the smoke jack, and of more modern introduction, the *propellers* designed by Mr. Taylor for the equipment of steam-boats, and which Mr. Green has availed himself of to shew the effect of atmospheric re-action in directing the course of the balloon. Now all these and similar expedients are merely modifications of the same principle, more or less perfect as they more or less resemble the perfect screw, but all falling far short of the efficacy of that instrument in its primitive character and construction. The reason of this deficiency can be readily accounted for. All the modifications alluded to, which have hitherto been applied to the purposes of locomotion, are adaptations of *plane* surfaces. Now it is the character of *plane* surfaces to present the same angle, and consequently to impinge upon the air with the same condition of obliquity throughout. But the *rate* of revolution, and consequently of impact, varies according to the distance from the axis; being greatest at the outer edge, and gradually diminishing as it approaches the centre of rotation, where it may be supposed to be altogether evanescent. Now it is by the re-action of the air against *one* side of the impinging plane, that the progressive motion is determined in the opposite direction, which re-action is proportioned to the *rate* of impact, the angle remaining the same. If then we suppose a re-action corresponding to the *greatest rate* of revolution, which is that due to the *outermost* portion of the impinging surface (that most removed from the axis of rotation) we shall have a *progressive* motion in the whole apparatus greater than the rate of impact of the *innermost* or more central portions of the revolving plane; and accordingly the re-action will be thereabouts transferred from the back to the front of the propulsive apparatus, and tend to retard instead of advancing the progress of the machine to which it is attached. This inconvenience is felt and acknowledged by all those who have employed this principle to obtain a progressive motion, and accordingly a provision has been made against it in the *removal* or *reduction* of the central portion of the revolving vanes, with a view to let the air escape or pass through as the instrument advances; a provision which is certainly effectual to that end, but at the cost of the *surface*, which is the ultimate source of the required re-action. All this is avoided in the use of the perfect screw. There, the rate of rotation and the angle of impact mutually corresponding, may be said to play into each other's hands; the spiral becoming more extended as the impact becomes less forcible, that is as it approaches the centre, where both altogether vanish or disappear; thus obviating the possibility of any interruption to the course of the machine from the contrarious impact of the air, however quick or however slow the motions, either of the screw itself or of the machine which is propelled by its operation. In attestation of this fact and as showing the immunity of the perfect screw from the disparaging effects experienced by the other modes of accomplishing the same object, I will only mention a circumstance related to me by Mr. Smith himself, to whom I am glad to acknowledge myself indebted for so much valuable information respecting this instrument, which, by the light he has thrown upon its use and the improvements he has introduced into its construction, he may be truly said to have made his own. Upon a late occasion, when trying one of the larger class of vessels which had just been furnished by him upon this principle, some persons not perceiving the true nature of the figure employed, contended that some opposition must be experienced by the central portion of the screw, which revolved so much less rapidly than the rate of the ship itself. In order to convince them of their error, Mr. Smith caused a portion of the surface in question, next the axis, to a certain distance, to be cut away, leaving an opening, by which, for the water to escape. The result was, immediately, the loss of one mile an hour in the rate of the ship; thus shewing that even the most apparently feeble portion of the impinging surface of this instrument contributes, in its degree, to the constitution of the aggregate force of which it is productive.

This peculiarity of construction is the main cause of the advantage which the Archimedean Screw possesses over all its types or imitations; but it is not the only one. The *entirety* or *unbroken continuity* of its surface is another, not much less influential. The value of this will be the more readily appreciated when we consider that air, unlike water and other non-elastic fluids, undergoes a rarefaction or impoverishment of density, and consequently of resisting power, accordingly as it is swept away by the rapid passage of impinging planes; the parts immediately *behind*, and to a considerable distance, being thereby relieved from the support they had previously experienced, and extending (and consequently becoming thinner) in order to fill up the space thus partially cleared away. Now it is evident that if other planes be brought into operation in the parts of the atmosphere thus impoverished, before they have had time to recover their pristine or natural density, they will of necessity act with diminished vigour; the resistance being ever proportioned to the density of the resisting medium. This is the condition into which, more or less, all systems of revolving planes are necessarily brought, that consist of more than one; and is a grand cause of the little real effect they have been made capable of producing, whenever tried. The nature of this objection, and the extent to which it operates, will appear most strikingly from the following fact. Mr. Henson's scheme of flight is founded upon the principle of an inclined plane, started from an eminence by an extrinsic force, applied and *continued* by the revolution of impinging vanes, in form and number resembling the sails of a windmill. In the experiments which were made in this gallery with several models of this proposed construction, it was found that so far from *aiding* the machine in its flight, the operation of these vanes actually *impeded* its progress; inasmuch as it was always found to proceed to a greater distance by the mere force of acquired velocity (which is the only force it ever displayed), than when the vanes were set in motion to aid it—a simple fact, which it is unnecessary to dilate upon. It is to the agency of this cause, namely, the broken continuity of surface, that, I have no doubt, is also to be ascribed the failure of the attempt of Sir George Cayley to propel a Balloon of a somewhat similar shape to the present, which he made at the Polytechnic Institution a short while since, when he employed a series of revolving vanes, four in number, disposed at proper intervals around, but which were found ineffectual to move it. Had these separate surfaces been thrown into *one*, of the nature and form of the Archimedean Screw, there is little doubt that the experiment would have been attended with a different result. In accordance with the principles here illustrated, the Archimedean Screw properly consists of only *one* turn; more than one being productive of no more resistance, and consequently superfluous. A single unbroken turn of the screw, however, when the diameter is of any magnitude, would require a considerable length of axis, which in its adaptation to the Balloon, would be practically objectionable; accordingly *two half turns*, nearly equivalent in power to one whole turn, has been preferred ; as in most instances it has been by Mr. Smith, himself, in his application of it to the navigation of the seas.

Indeed, in all other respects, except the nature of its material, the screw here represented is exactly analogous to that used by Mr. Smith in its most perfect form, having been, in fact, designed, and in part constructed under his own supervision.*

The model upon which these principles have been now, for the first time, successfully, at least, tried in the air, is constructed upon the following scale. The Balloon is, as before stated, an ellipsoid or solid oval; in length, 13 feet 6 inches, and in height, 6 feet 8 inches. It contains, accordingly, a volume of gas equal to about 320 cubic feet, which, in pure hydrogen, would enable it to support a weight of twenty-one pounds, which is about its real power when recently inflated, and before the gas has had time to become deteriorated by the process of *endosmose*.† The whole weight of the machine and apparatus is seventeen pounds; consequently there is about four pounds to spare, in order to meet this contingency.

* The frame was made at Mr. Smith's request, by Mr. Pilgrim, of the Archimedes; the original experimental vessel in which this mode of propulsion was first tried upon the large scale. Mr. Pilgrim has been long versed in all that relates to the mechanism of this instrument, and is indeed a most expert and ingenious artist.

† *Endosmose* is that operation by which gases of different specific gravities are enabled, or rather forced to come together through the pores of any membranous or other flexible covering by which it is sought to restrain them. As above referred to, it is the introduction of atmospheric air into the body of the Balloon through the pores of the silk, however accurately varnished, by which the purity of the hydrogen gas is contaminated, and its buoyant power ultimately exhausted. This it is impossible to prevent by any process, except the interposition of a *metallic* covering; as for instance, by *gilding* the Balloon, which would be effectual could it be contrived to endure the constant friction and bending of the material itself.

Beneath the centre of the Balloon, and about two-thirds of its length, is a frame of light wood, answering to the hoop of an ordinary Balloon ; to which are attached the cords of the net which encloses the suspending vessel, and which serves to distribute the pressure of the appended weight equally over its whole surface, as well as to form an intermediate means of attachment for the rest of the apparatus. This consists of a car or basket in the centre ; at one end the rudder, and at the other the Archimedean Screw. The car is about two feet long and eighteen inches broad, and is laced to the hoop by cords, which running through loops instead of being fastened individually, allow of unlimited play, and equalize the application of the weight of the car to the hoop, as of the whole to the Balloon above. The Archimedean Screw consists of an axis of hollow brass tube eighteen inches in length, through which, upon a semi-spiral of 15° of inclination, are passed a series of radii or spokes of steel wire, two feet long, (thus projecting a foot on either side) and which being connected at their outer extremities by two bands of flattened wire, form the frame work of the Screw, which is completed by a covering of oiled silk cut into gores, and tightly stretched, so as to present as nearly uniform a surface as the nature of the case will permit. This Screw is supported at either end of the axis by pillars of hollow brass tube descending from the hoop, in the lower extremities of which are the holes in which the pivots of the axis revolve. From the end of the axis which is next the car, proceeds a shaft of steel, which connects the Archimedean Screw with the pinion of a piece of spring machinery seated in the car ; by the operation of which it is made to revolve, and a progressive motion communicated to the whole apparatus. This spring is of considerable power compared with its dimensions, being capable of raising about 45 pounds upon a barrel of four inches diameter after the first turn, and gradually increasing as it is wound up. It weighs altogether, eight pounds six ounces.

The rudder is a light frame of cane covered with silk, somewhat of the form of an elongated battledoor, about three feet long, and one foot wide, where it is largest. It might be made considerably larger if required, being exceedingly light and yet sufficiently strong for any force to which it could be subjected. It weighs altogether only two ounces and a half. This instrument possesses a double character. Besides its proper purpose of guiding the horizontal course of the Balloon, it is capable of being applied in a novel manner to its elevation or depression, when driven by the propulsive power of the Screw. Being so contrived as to be capable of being turned *flat*, and also directed upwards or downwards as well as to the right or left, it enables the aeronaut to transfer the resistance of the air, which, in any inclined position, it must generate in its passage, to any side upon which he may desire to act, and thus give a determination to the course of the Balloon in the opposite direction. This will appear more clear as well as more certain when we consider, that the aerial vessel being in a state of perfect equipoise, as it ever must be when proceeding on the same level, the slightest alteration in its buoyancy is sufficient to send it to a considerable distance either up or down as the case may be: the rejection of a pound of ballast, or of an equivalent amount of gas, being enough to conduct the aeronaut to the extremest limits of his desires in either direction, whatever may be the size of his Balloon. Now a resistance equal to many pounds is attainable by an inclined plane of even moderate dimensions when propelled even with moderate velocity; and being readily governed by the mere inclination of the impinging plane at the will and by the hand of the aerial voyager, it will be in his power to vary the level of his machine with very considerable nicety; enabling him to approach the surface of the earth, or in a gentle curve to sweep away from its occasional irregularities, and proceed to a very considerable elevation without interrupting the progress of his course, and, what is of more importance, without sacrificing any part of his resources in gas or ballast, upon the preservation of which the duration of his career so entirely depends. These properties of the rudder it is not possible to display in the present exhibition, owing to the confined nature of the course which it is necessary to pursue; but they were sufficiently tested in the preliminary experiments at Willis's Rooms, where the space being larger, a circular motion was conferred upon the machine by connecting it with a fixed centre round which it was thus made to revolve, without the necessity of confining it to the one level.

The rate of motion which the Balloon thus equipped is capable of accomplishing varies according to the circumstances of its propulsion. When the Archimedean Screw precedes, the velocity is less than when it is made to follow, owing to the reaction of the air in the former instance against the car, the under surface of the balloon, and other obstacles, by which its progress is retarded. Again, when the cord upon which it travels is most tense and free from vibration, the rate is found to be considerably accelerated, compared with what it is when the contrary conditions prevail. But chiefly is its speed affected by the proper *ballasting* of the machine itself, upon which depends the friction it encounters from the cord on which it travels. Under ordinary circumstances it proceeds at a rate of about four miles an hour, but when the conditions alluded to have been most favourable, it has accomplished a velocity of not less than five; and there is no doubt that were it altogether free from restraint, as it would be in the open air, with a hand to guide it, its progress would be upwards of six miles an hour.

Having now, I trust, sufficiently explained the principles exemplified in the model here described, it may be expected that I should add a few words regarding their reduction into practice upon a larger scale and in the open air, with such difficulties to contend with as may be expected to be encountered in the prosecution of such a design. In the first place, however, it will be necessary to disabuse the public mind of some very prevailing misconceptions with respect to the conditions of a Balloon exposed to the action of the winds, pursuing its course under the exercise of an inherent propulsive power. These misconceptions, which, be it observed, are more or less equally participated in by the scientific as by the ignorant, when devoid of that practical experience which is the basis of all aeronautical proficiency, are of a very vague and general character, and consequently not very easy accurately to define. In order, therefore, to make sure of meeting all the objections and removing all the doubts to which they are calculated to give rise, it will be advisable, even at the risk of a little tediousness, to separate them into distinct questions and treat them accordingly.

One of the most specious of these misconceptions regards the effects of the resistance of the atmosphere upon the figure of the Balloon when rapidly propelled through the air, whereby it is presumed its opposing front will be driven in, and more or less incapacitated from performing the part assigned to it; namely, to cleave its way with the reduced resistance due to its proper form. To obviate this imagined result, various remedies have been proposed—such as, to construct that part of the machine of more solid materials than the rest, or else (as suggested by one of the most scientific and ingenious of those who have devoted their attention to the theory of aerial navigation), to subject the gaseous contents of the Balloon to such a degree of artificial condensation by compression, as shall supply from within a force equal to that from without; adopting, of course, materials of a stronger texture than those at present in use, for the construction of the balloon. Now the contingency against which it is here sought to provide, and which I grant is a very reasonable one to anticipate, has nevertheless no real existence in practice; at least in such a degree as to render it necessary to have recourse to any particular expedient for its prevention. Taking it for granted that the hypothesis in which it is involved is founded upon a presumed analogy with a Balloon exposed to the action of the wind while in a state of attachment to the earth, I would first observe that the cases in question, however apparently analogous, are in reality essentially dissimilar. In the one case (that where the Balloon is supposed to be attached to the earth) all the *motion*, and consequently all the *momentum*, is in the air; in the other case (where the Balloon is supposed to be progressive), it is in the constituent particles of the machine itself and of its gaseous contents. And this momentum, which is ever proportioned to the rate of its motion, and, consequently, to the amount of resistance it experiences, is amply sufficient to secure the preservation of the form of its opposing front, however partially distended, and whatever the velocity with which it might happen to be endowed. Independently, however, of this corrective principle, another, equally efficacious is afforded in the buoyant power of the included gas, which, occupying all the upper part of the Balloon so long as it is in a condition to sustain itself in the air, and generally extending to its whole capacity, presses from within with a force far greater than any it could experience from the external impact of the atmosphere, and sufficiently resists any impression from that quarter which might tend to impair its form. To what extent this is effective, will appear more clearly when we observe that in any balloon inflated, it is the *sides* of the distended globe that bear out the weight of the appended cargo, through the intervention of the network; a weight only limited by the sustaining power of the machine itself, and in the case of the great Vauxhall or Nassau Balloon, amounting to more than two tons, and consequently pressing with a force far exceeding any that could arise from the impact of the air at any rate of motion it could ever be expected to accomplish. And this statement, which represents the theoretical view of the question, is fully borne out by the real circumstances of the case as they appear in practice. So far from justifying the apprehensions of those who conceive that the *front* of the Balloon would be disfigured by its compulsory progression through the air, the result is exactly the reverse; the only tendency to derangement of form displaying itself in the part *behind*, where the rushing in of the atmospheric medium to fill the place of the advancing body (in the nature of an *eddy*, as it is termed in water), might and no doubt would, to some extent (though perhaps but slightly) affect the figure of that part, in a manner, however, calculated rather to aid than to impair the general design in view.

Another error of more universal prevalency, because of a more superficial character, regards the condition of the Balloon as affected by the currents of air, in and through which it might have to be propelled. The arguments founded upon such a view of the case, generally assume some such form as the following—" It is true you can accomplish such or such a rate of motion; but that is only in a room, with a calm atmosphere, or with a favourable current of wind. In the open air, with the wind at the rate of twenty or thirty miles an hour, your feeble power would be of no avail. You could never expect to direct your course *against* the wind, and if you were to attempt it and the wind were strong, you would inevitably be blown to pieces by the force of the current." Now this argument is equally nought with the preceding. The condition of the Balloon, as far as regards the exercise of its propulsive powers, is precisely the same whether the wind be strong or gentle, with it or against it. In neither case would the Balloon experience any opposition or resistance to its progress but what *itself*, by its *own* independent motion, created; and that opposition or resistance would be exactly the same in whatever direction it might be sought to be established. The Balloon, passively suspended in the air, without the exercise of a propulsive power, experiences no effects whatever from the motion of the atmosphere in which it is carried, however violent; and the establishment of such a propulsive power could never subject it to more than the force itself, with which it was invested. The *way* which the Balloon so provided would make through the air would always be the same, in whatever direction, or with whatever violence the wind might happen to blow; and the condition of the Balloon would always be the same that was due to its *own independent* rate of motion, without regard to any other circumstances whatever. If it was furnished with the means of accomplishing a rate of motion equal to ten miles an hour, it would experience a certain amount of atmospheric resistance due to that rate; and this amount of resistance with all its concomitant consequences, neither more nor less, would it experience, whether it endeavoured to make this way *against* a wind blowing at the rate of 100 miles an hour, or *with* the same in its favour. The result, so far as regards its distance from the place of starting, would, I grant, be very different; but at present we are only considering the conditions of its motion through the *air*, and these, I repeat, would be the same whatever the rate or course of the wind; so that all speculations on this score must resolve themselves into questions of *quantity*, not of *quality*, in the effect sought to be accomplished: in other words, all consideration of the rate of the wind must be left out of the argument, except, in so far as it shall be taken to regulate the limit which shall be assigned to the rate of the aerial machine, as sufficient to justify its claims to the title of a successful mode of navigating the skies.*

* The condition of a Balloon propelled by machinery is very analogous to that of a boat in the water driven by oars or paddles. Suppose such a boat to be rowing or paddling up a river against the stream, if a piece of cork be thrown overboard it appears to be carried away with the current. But this is delusive; it is the boat *alone* which really moves away from the cork. For if the boat be left to its own course,

With these conditions established, it will now be seen that we have nothing to consider, in discussing the probable success of any scheme of aerial navigation with the aid of the Balloon (so far as its mere movements are concerned)* except the *actual rate of motion* which it is competent to accomplish; whether or not it be sufficient to meet the exigencies of the case as they may happen to be estimated. That its capabilities in that respect, be displayed within a room, or in a calm atmosphere, or under what may be called the most favourable circumstances, has nothing in it to disparage or affect the general question.

both it and the cork will float down together; and if the use of the oars or paddles be resumed, the distance between the boat and the cork will proceed to develope itself exactly according to the rate of the *boat*, without any regard to that of the *stream*. If the stream be excessively rapid, the boatsmen will appear to be exercising very great force to enable them to stem the torrent and avoid being carried backward. Now the resistance which they experience and all its attendant effects are only those which they create for themselves, and which they would experience in exactly the same degree were they to endeavour to move *at the same rate* in calm water or with the current in their favour. If the current be at the rate of ten miles an hour and they are just able to maintain their place, they are proceeding at the rate of ten miles an hour, and they experience the opposition due to that rate of motion; precisely the same as they would experience if they sought to accomplish the same rate of motion under any other circumstances. And if the current were 100 miles an hour, they would suffer no more from endeavouring to go against it, with the force just ascribed to them, than if they were to exercise the same force in any other direction, or in a water perfectly tranquil. Apply this reasoning to the case of a Balloon propelled by machinery, and much of the obscurity in which it is involved will disappear.

* I have said "so far as its mere movements are concerned;" because the complete success of the scheme, how far it is an available and satisfactory mode of transport, depends upon other conditions besides the accomplishment of a given rate of motion—as for instance, whether it be safe, or practicable, or consistent with a due preservation of the *buoyancy* of the Balloon, so as to allow of its being employed in voyages of sufficient distance and duration, or capable of being worked at moderate cost, or whether it leave sufficient allowance for cargo; with many others of less striking importance, which the practical aeronaut will readily suggest for himself.

Whatever it can do *there*, it can do the same in a hurricane; and the only real question is, "whether, what it *can* accomplish in respect of rate, is enough to answer the purpose in view."

The model we have been just describing is capable as we have seen, of accomplishing a rate of about six miles an hour. Now the resistance to the progress of a Balloon varies as the squares of the velocities or rates of motion. Accordingly, for the same Balloon to accomplish twice the speed, or twelve miles an hour, it would be necessary to be provided with four times the power. Thus as the spring power employed in the model is equal to a weight of 45 pounds, upon a barrel of four inches in diameter, it would require one competent to raise 180 pounds on the same sized barrel, to enable it to propel the same Balloon at double the present rate.

But with regard to Balloons of different sizes and of the same shape, the power required to produce the same rate of motion, would be as the squares of their respective diameters: for the power is as the resistance, the resistance as the surface, and the surface follows the proportion just assigned. In order, therefore, to propel a Balloon of the same form and twice the diameter, at the same rate, it would require a force of four times the amount.

Now to apply this to the consideration of a Balloon of superior magnitude, let us assume one of 100 feet in length, and fifty feet in height. The buoyant power of such a machine, or the weight it would carry, supposing it inflated with gas of the same specific gravity, compared with that of the model, would be as the cubes of their respective diameters; or in, about, the ratio of 420 to one. Such a Balloon, therefore, so inflated, would carry a weight of about 8700 pounds, or above three tons and three quarters. As, however, it would be very expensive to inflate such a vessel with pure hydrogen gas, it would be advisable to found our calculations upon the use of coal gas; under which circumstances the weight it would carry would be limited to about three tons. Deducting from this, one ton for the weight of the Balloon itself and its necessary equipments, there would remain two tons, or about 4500 pounds, to be devoted to the power, whatever it might be, by which the machinery was to be moved, and the living cargo it might have to carry. Nor let the reader be surprised at the magnitude of the figures we are here employing, as if it were something extraordinary, or beyond the power of man to accomplish. The dimensions and power we have here assumed is very little greater than those of the great Vauxhall Balloon,* and considerably less than some of *Montgolfières*, or Fire-balloons, which were first employed.

Now the resistance which such a Balloon as I have here described would experience in its passage through the air, and consequently the power it would require to establish that resistance, compared with those of the model, we have said would be as the *squares* of their respective diameters, or in, about, the ratio of only fifty-six to one; in other words, whatever force it would take to propel the model at any given rate, it would require just fifty-six times the power to accomplish the same result with the large Balloon we have been describing.

In order to ascertain precisely what this power would be in any given instance, it only remains to find an expression for the spring power with which we have been hitherto dealing, that shall be more generally comprehensible.

This we shall do by a comparison with the power of steam, according to the usual mode of estimating it; that is, reckoning a one-horse power to be equal to the traction or draught of 32,000 lbs. through the space of one foot in a minute. According to this scale, observing the corresponding conditions of the spring—namely, the weight it balances on the barrel, (answering to the force of traction) = 45 lbs., the circumference

* The height of the Vauxhall Balloon is about eighty feet, its breadth about fifty. It contains 85000 cubic feet of gas, and supports a weight of upwards of two tons.

of the barrel (answering to the space traversed) = one foot, and the time of uncoiling for each turn, (answering to the rate of the operation) say, three seconds and a half—we find the power of the spring employed in the propulsion of the model, to be as nearly as possible the forty-second part of the power of one horse; from whence it is easy to deduce the conditions of flight assignable to the same, and to different sized Balloons of the same shape, at any other degree of speed. Assuming, for instance, a Balloon of 100 feet in length and 50 feet in height, and proposing a rate of motion equal to 20 miles an hour, we have, in the first instance, the power required to propel the model at that rate, compared with that already ascertained for a velocity of six miles an hour, in the ratio of the *squares of the two velocities*, as nearly ten to one; that is, ten forty-seconds, or about one-fourth of a horse power. To apply this to the larger Balloon, we must take the squares of their respective diameters; which being nearly in the ratio of 56 to 1, gives an amount of 56 times one-fourth or about 14 horses, as the sum of the power required.

From what particular source the power to be employed in the propulsion of the Balloon should be deduced, is not indeed a question without some difficulties and doubts in the determination. To all the moving powers at present before the world some objections apply which disparage their application, or altogether exclude them from our consideration.

The power of the coiled spring is too limited to be employed upon a larger scale. The use of the steam-engine is accompanied with a gradual consumption of the resources of the Balloon in ballast, and consequently in gas, the one being exactly answerable to the other, and is therefore not calculated for voyages of long duration. Human strength appears to be too feeble for great results, and moreover, requires repose; which reduces the amount assignable to each man to a fraction of its nominal value. Of electro-magnetism as yet we know too little to enable us to pronounce upon it with certainty. Of the remaining powers known only one is worth mentioning in connexion with this subject, namely, the elastic force of air; and this I only mention because it has been taken up by one whose authority in these matters is deservedly entitled to much weight, and who entertains great hopes of making it ultimately subservient to the purpose in view.

But although none of these powers, in their present state, be so perfectly adapted to the propulsion of the Balloon as to leave nothing further to desire, yet are some of them so far applicable as, undoubtedly, to enable us to accomplish, by their means, a very large amount of success. A steam engine of the power required, namely, equal to fourteen horses, could be easily constructed, far within the limits of weight which we have at our disposal upon that account in the Balloon under consideration, or even in one much smaller; and recent improvements have so far reduced the amount of coal required for its maintenance, that perhaps as long a voyage could be made by means of it now, as would be expected or required. Even human strength, by a certain mode of applying it, might be made effectual to the accomplishment of a very sufficient rate of motion, say fourteen or fifteen miles an hour, for, continuously, as long a period as the natural strength of man, moderately taxed, could endure, and which we may reckon at twelve hours.

It is true that neither the velocity here quoted, nor that before assumed is so great as to enable the aeronaut to compete with some of the modes of transit employed on the surface of the earth; as, for instance, the railroads, where 25 miles an hour is not an unusual speed. Yet is not the aerial machine which could command such a rate of motion to be despised, or set aside as inferior in actual accomplishments to what is already at our disposal; for it must not be lost sight of, that railroads, or terrestrial roads of every description, must ever be limited in their extent and direction, and travelling on them, however perfectly contrived, subject to deviations and interruptions, particularly in passing from one country to another beyond the seas, which if taken into account, would reduce the apparent estimate of their rates, considerably under the lowest of those assigned to the Balloon in the previous calculation ; and at all events, by sea, much less, under the most favourable circumstances, is the ordinary rate of ships.

But, it may be observed, we are here counting upon a rate of motion as established, which is only effectual to that extent in the absence of contrary currents of wind. This is true; nevertheless, it is no bar to the use which might be made of the aerial conveyance so furnished, nor any disparagement to the advantages which might be drawn from it; for not only does the aeronaut possess the means of choosing, within certain limits, the currents to which he may please to commit himself, and of which, abundance of every variety is sure to be met with at some elevation or other in the atmosphere, but, as in all general arguments, where the conditions are equally applicable to both sides of the question, they may be fairly left out as neutralising each other, so, here it must not be forgotten, that the currents in question, being altogether indeterminate, and equally to be expected from all quarters, an equal chance exists of advantages to be derived, as of disadvantages to be encountered from their occurrence; and that, even without the means of making a selection, the admitted laws of reasoning would justify us in considering the chances of the latter to be fully counterbalanced by those of the former. It is enough, for moderate success at least, if, possessing the power of avoiding the bad, and of availing himself of the good, the aeronaut be furnished with the means of making a sufficient progress for himself, when the atmosphere is such as neither to favour nor to obstruct him; and in this condition I humbly conceive he would be placed, with even a less rate of motion than that which we have before assigned, and confidently reckon upon being able to accomplish.

FINIS.

www.ingramcontent.com/pod-product-compliance
Lightning Source LLC
LaVergne TN
LVHW011122110826
845150LV00008B/2220

9781418195601